BARRON'S

D0108264

Katrin Behrend

kovics

CONTENTS

TYPICAL CAT

- Soft and cuddly

- Happy to be petted and carried around

- Shows contentment by purring

- Strong-willed, independent, and inaccessible

- Endowed with sharp teeth and claws

- Capable of scratching, biting, hissing, and shrieking in self-defense

- Excellent hunter

- Enjoys eating mice

- Nimble climber and extremely sure-footed

- Certain to land on its feet

The ancestors of our house cats were the tawny cats once indigenous to North Africa. In the new kingdom of the Egyptians, grain supplies were stored in immense granaries that swarmed with rats and mice. Since the tawny cats were attracted to the bounty of this hunting ground, they came into contact with humans who esteemed and admired them; therefore, the cats stayed and practically domesticated themselves.

The evolution of cats has been marked by many changes. They began their conquest of the world in Egypt, where they were revered as representatives of their gods, but then their fortune waned. In medieval Europe they fell victim to the absurd stories surrounding witchcraft. Not until the seventeenth century did people again recognize their good points; this appreciation has continued to this day.

IS A CAT FOR YOU?

1 A cat can live to be 15 to 20 years old. That's how long you'll be responsible for the animal.

2 A cat needs regular vaccinations, which cost money, in addition to your expenses for food and upkeep.

3 Depending on the type of fur, cats shed hair on rugs and furniture and regurgitate the hair they swallow when they groom themselves. They spread litter and droppings around their litterbox. You will need patience.

4 Cats cannot be trained the way dogs can, and they are especially independent, something you have to accept.

5 A cat that lives only indoors needs a lot of attention and activity. Can you provide that?

6 Even if your cat is a gift to your child, you will probably still have to get involved with its care.

7 Do you have any other house pets that a cat might not get along with (see page 28)?

8 What will happen to the cat while you're away on vacation or perhaps ill?

9 Have you consulted with your landlord and neighbors? Usually it's permissible to keep a cat in rented quarters as long as you make sure it causes no damage.

10 If you or any other family member is allergic to animal hair, you should not own a cat.

One Cat or Two?

Cats are happy being only pets and often go off on their own, but they always come back, and they remain devoted to their humans. If you're at work during the day and can't be with your cat, it may be a good idea to get two cats. If they get along, they'll keep each other company, play together, cuddle, and engage in minor skirmishes with one another.

Possibilities include:

✔ Two females from the same litter
✔ An older and a younger cat
✔ Two grown cats, but they must carefully grow accustomed to one another, and they need enough space so that each one can stake out its own territory (see page 28).

PURCHASE AND ADJUSTMENT

Living with a cat involves accepting inconsistency and alternating between affection and wildness, accessibility and reserve, affection and distance. One moment a cat may be clinging; shortly thereafter, it may be indifferent to a person's feelings.

From Wild Cat to House Cat

The history of the house cat is comparatively short, since it took longer to become domesticated than any other house pet. It's been about 4,000 years since the cat came to our attention and established its reputation for both its beauty and its unsurpassed skill as a mouse catcher. When the tawny wild cats that had been living in Northern Africa *(Felis lybica)*—slender animals with large ears and a long tail—joined with humans, there arose the so-called cost and benefit principle: Cats killed the rats and mice that had infested the huge granaries, and humans appreciated and rewarded them for that with care and attention. One might say that the domestication of cats was their own doing; they willingly gave themselves over to the care of humans. Cats have been content to live with humans, but to this day they have kept their independence.

House cats first came to Central Europe at the time of the Carolingians around 800 A.D.

The Carthusian is aloof and won't submit to being carried around all the time.

and mixed freely with the indigenous wild cats of the forest *(Felis silvestris)*. This didn't produce a blending of both breeds, however, as kittens from such breeding pairs usually are not able to be tamed. On the other hand, wild cats with the aptitude of a house cat would not survive in the wild.

House cats have retained many qualities of their wild ancestry and still share them with their wild relatives; in fact, the cat family *(Felidae)* constitutes a very unified group. Every cat, whether big or small, is unmistakably feline and cannot be mistaken for any other animal.

Origin of Breeds

We owe the first breeds to mutations—sudden changes in hereditary makeup. In one instance there appears a different color, in another, long hair or a delicate physique. Among these original breeds are the Maine Coon and the Norwegian Forest Cat. Also included in this group is the Turkish Angora, one of the world's oldest breeds of cat.

These early cats lived in a geographically isolated region and could multiply only within their own breed; therefore, they consolidated the characteristic qualities of the oriental

This Burmese, like every cat, is a hunter.

long-haired cats without any intervention on the part of humans.

Among these cats, which were usually white, several types arose over time and were further propagated. People came to prefer cats with a compact physique, a broader head, and a flatter face, leading to the intentional breeding of Persian cats.

Systematic cat breeding has been practiced for about 100 years, as follows:

✔ Choices are not made on the basis of efficiency, but rather according to appearance and emotional needs.

✔ The variety of colors and types made it possible to establish traits that characterize each breed and remain constant.

✔ Without knowledge of Mendel's laws of inherited traits, purposeful breeding was not possible. Those laws were eventually amplified and successfully applied, as we can see by the results.

What Is a Standard?

The defining traits of an "ideal" animal of any breed are put in writing in a standard, which refers specifically to appearance and to desired features. Today, about 50 breeds are recognized; their standards are judged and given awards by several organizations (see Information, page 62). The following descriptions of individual breeds provide only a glimpse. For detailed characteristics, consult your pet store owner, breeder, or the ample specialty publications that are available.

Individual Breeds

Persian and Exotic Cats

All have a powerful physique, short, strong legs, a rounded head, small ears, big round eyes, and a short, stubby nose with the typical *break* or *stop*, the indentation between forehead and tip of the nose. The fur is long, thick, and fine; eye color can be orange or copper, green, blue, or varied. Coat color and pattern are diverse, with presently over 200 variations. These include single-colored, multicolored, colorpoint, flowing, smoked, shaded, and tipped.

Long-haired Cats

These breeds sport long, flowing fur, but don't have the typical flat face of Persian cats. They include the Angora, Balinese, Birman, Javanese, Maine Coon Cat, Norwegian Forest Cat, Ragdoll, Somali, and Turkish Van.

Short-haired Cats

There are several breeds whose only common characteristic is short fur. In appearance they can range from powerful and ungainly to elegant, slender, and delicate. These include the Abyssinian, Bengal, British Shorthair, British Short-

hair Blue (Carthusian), Burmese, Chartreux, European Shorthair, Havana, Japanese Bobtailed Cat, Manx, Rex, Russian Blue, Scottish Fold, and Tonkinese.

Siamese and Oriental Shorthaired Cats

These especially slender, delicate cats are distinguished by an elongated head with a straight profile. The slightly bent tail, once typical for Siamese, today is regarded as a defect.

The Traditional Siamese, or Old Style Siamese, has a rounder head and heavier body than does the Extreme Siamese, whose sleek, elegant appearance is favored today in the show ring. Fanciers of the Traditional Siamese believe that it is closer to the original type that existed before humans began to experiment with it. On the other hand, Extreme Siamese fanciers think that their cat's was the original look, altered in the early years of the breed.

The Oriental Shorthair has a body type like that of the Siamese, but, whereas the Siamese has only light hair with dark points, the Oriental Shorthair comes in a wide variety of colors.

Known for their playfulness and intelligence, both breeds are ideal companions.

With tail held high and resolute steps, the cat approaches its owner.

CAT PROFILES

Abyssinian wild-colored male, one year old.

Bengal black-spotted male, two years old.

Birman bluepoint, seven weeks old.

Abyssinians

They are among the oldest breeds and most closely resemble their ancestors, the African tawny cats.

✔ Medium-sized, slender, elegant. Eyes green to gold-colored. Short, thick coat (banding of individual hairs).

✔ Wild-colored, sorrel, blue, beige-fawn, silver.

✔ Friendly, receptive, intelligent. Like to climb and romp. Need exercise.

✔ A good choice for people who can devote time and attention to them.

Bengals

Bengals were developed from wild cats.

✔ Medium to large size, muscular, lithe. Green or gold eyes. Short, thick fur.

✔ Primary colors: from sandy to golden to reddish orange.

✔ Intelligent, receptive. Exceptional climbers that need lots of exercise.

✔ A good choice for family cats, as they are sturdy, unspoiled, and devoted.

Note: When you acquire one of these cats, be sure that it's sufficiently domesticated and accustomed to people.

Birmans

These are presumed to be a cross between Siamese and Persians.

✔ Strong and muscular, medium to long fur. Deep blue eyes. Distinguishing feature: white paws.

✔ Light beige body; darker-colored face, ears, paws, and tail (Siamese); usually sealpoint (brown) and bluepoint (blue).

✔ In temperament, a combination of the lively Siamese and the subdued Persian. Endearing, friendly, and sociable.

✔ A good choice for families with children; ideal for apartments, as they don't need to go outdoors.

Male Burmese bluepoint.
Needs close contact with its owner.

British Shorthair blue male,
2½ years old.

Burmese chocolate female,
7 months old.

Maine Coon, creme tabby
male, three years old.

British Shorthair Blue

Carthusian, bred from a combination of English house cats and Persians; one of the most beloved breeds.

✔ Medium to large size, solid. Broad head with large cheeks. Yellow-orange to copper-colored or green eyes. Short, thick, velvety fur.

✔ Uniform light gray, designated as blue.

✔ Friendly, self-assured, and even-tempered.

✔ Gets along fine with children and other house pets and are ideal cats for apartment living.

Burmese

This breed was developed in 1930 in the United States by crossing a female Burmese cat with a male Siamese.

✔ Medium size, slender, powerful. Indented nose, pale yellow to amber-colored eyes. Short, fine, silky fur.

✔ Brown, blue, champagne, creme, lilac, red, chocolate, sealpoint, bluepoint, and lilac-tortie.

✔ Self-assured, likes to be in charge. Rides well in the car and likes to travel.

✔ Needs people who want a sensible, confident cat and have lots of time to devote to it.

Maine Coon

This primitive breed comes from Maine, where it once lived in the wild.

✔ Large, solid, muscular. Ears have thick tufts of hair. Green or gold-orange eyes. Long, thick, water-repellent fur with full ruff.

✔ All colors and markings except Siamese points, chocolate, and lilac.

✔ Well adjusted, sociable, and easygoing.

✔ Robust, easy-to-care-for longhaired cats that get along well with children.

Carthusian,
four months old
(right); Maine
Coon, red classic
tabby, seven
weeks old (left).

Norwegian Forest Cat, black and white.

Oriental Shorthair Havana female, two years old.

Persian black female, two years old.

Norwegian Forest Cat

A primitive breed from Norway that developed through natural selection.

✔ Medium-sized, powerful, lithe. Nose and ears form a triangle. Long, thick, water-repellent fur.

✔ Any color possible.

✔ Friendly, lively, playful. Likes to climb and cuddle.

✔ Needs to be around people and likes children.

Oriental Shorthair

These cats are actually pro-totypical Siamese of all one color, without the typical Siamese points.

✔ Medium-sized, lanky, and slender. Wedge-shaped head. Green eyes. Very short fur, finely textured and smooth.

✔ Examples include Havana, Blue, Ebony, Red, and many others.

✔ Temperamental and playful; needs plenty of opportunities to climb and scratch.

✔ Good for people who have experience with cats and can give them time and affection.

Persian

Their formula for success is a mixture of a baby face, big, wide eyes, and long, soft fur.

✔ Large, stocky, powerful. Broad head, pug nose. Copper, green, or blue eyes, or odd-eyed (two different colors). Long fur.

✔ Over 200 different colors and patterns.

✔ Calm, affectionate, gregarious.

✔ Ideal cat for family and apartment. Must be brushed and combed every day.

Persian, blue, smoked, nine weeks old. (right) Male Persian, colorpoint, bluepoint, fifteen months old.

Ragdoll seal-mitted male, four years old.

Siamese sealpoint female, five years old.

Turkish Van. Male, odd-eyed, one year old.

Ragdoll

This is quite a new breed; presumably it was produced from Persian Bicolors, Colorpoints, and Birmans.

✔ Medium-sized to large, powerful, muscular. Broad, wedge-shaped head. Nose with moderate break. Glowing blue eyes. Medium-long, velvety fur.

✔ Colorpoint frost, blue, chocolate, and sealpoint, bicolor, and mitted.

✔ Very gentle, composed, and patient. Ideal for apartment living.

✔ A good choice for families with children, other cats, and house pets.

Peculiarity: When Ragdoll cats are picked up, they let their head and paws droop down, which is the reason for their name.

Siamese

The Siamese cat comes from Bangkok; it first went to Europe about 100 years ago.

✔ Slender, delicate. Wedge-shaped head, long, straight nose. Blue eyes. Thick, fine-textured, very short fur.

✔ Many colors. Face, ears, paws, and tail are darker colored (Siamese points).

✔ Very temperamental, active, and fond of exercise. Exceptionally talkative.

✔ Needs people with experience and lots of feeling for cats.

Ragdoll seal bicolor female, four years old. A truly delightful cat.

Turkish Van

Comes from the mountains around the Van Lake in Turkey.

✔ Medium-sized, muscular. Likes water and swimming.

✔ White with spots on face and chestnut-colored tail.

✔ Freedom-loving cat that needs lots of room; likes attention with no obligations.

Choosing and Buying

Character is more important than appearance; take this into account before you fall for a specific kitten.

House Cat or Purebred?

With or without pedigree, cats are always beautiful. For someone who's simply interested in any kind of cat, it may make no difference whether it's a common house cat or a purebred. House cats are all common cats that are not bred according to any guidelines. They come in all colors and types of fur; they may be plump or slender, temperamental or calm—look only for the kind of cat that suits your taste (see Choosing the Right Cat, page 17).

A purebred cat is the result of years of care in breeding. For such feline beauty, the cost may range between $250 and $1,000. Even though the different breeds are less distinct from one another than breeds of dogs are, they still exhibit distinguishing traits, so don't just fall in love with appearance; also learn about the temperament and the traits of the various breeds (see pages 12 through 15).

Male or Female?

I have not been able to discern any fundamental sex-specific differences in behavior in my own cats. Any traits are more a function of their personalities than of their sex.

Consider that a female cat reaches sexual maturity between the ages of six and twelve months, and then comes into heat—becomes receptive to mating—two or three times a year. If a cat runs free, she can have many litters of kittens. On the other hand, in a situation where no male cat is available, feline heat cycles recur at frequent intervals.

A male cat becomes sexually mature around the age of nine months, and then marks its territory by spraying urine everywhere, creating foul odors indoors.

Note: When animals are neutered, their sexual desire leaves them, and the problems sometimes disappear completely (see page 36).

Everything is a toy for a young cat. If something in the box rustles and crackles, the curiosity is doubly strong.

Choosing the Right Cat

Kittens: Whether you are looking for a house cat or a purebred, you should approach the kitten of your choice with deliberation. Take time and look for an opportunity to observe the mother cat in her surroundings and how she behaves with her human. If she trusts that person, that's also impressed on her young. Track the development of the kittens in order to form an idea of what each one is like. Which one asserts itself in tussles around the milk bowl? Does it use the litterbox? How friendly is it toward visitors?

Cats from an animal shelter: If you are considering adopting an abandoned animal, find out as much as possible about its past. Notice whether the cat hisses or flees rather than coming up to you when you approach it.

Stray cats: Sometimes cats search for a home for themselves; suddenly, there's a cat at your door begging for food. These cats may not remain affectionate and friendly for very long, as they often have had to rely on themselves for months at a time and have taken on wild mannerisms. Try to win the trust of the cat by regularly setting out food which, of course, takes time. As soon as the cat allows itself to be touched, you should have it vaccinated and wormed by the veterinarian.

Note: Not every cat that crosses your path is abandoned, even if it looks ragged; you can't simply take it in. Always try to locate the owner, report your find to the local animal shelter, and provide the tattoo code if there's one. (See page 27).

What to Look for in a Cat

Healthy kittens play and romp a lot and fall into a deep sleep between periods of play. They are cautious with strangers, but still curious. Sick kittens, on the other hand, sit around pas-sively and are sometimes totally apathetic. Also look for:

✔ clean, soft fur with no knots and matting
✔ clear, shiny eyes
✔ clean ears with no secretions
✔ a dry nose with no discharge
✔ white teeth and pink gums
✔ clean area around the anus
✔ a tummy that is neither fat nor distended
✔ a generally well-padded body

Cat Supplies

Before you bring the cat home, you should have everything set up so that it will soon feel at home.

TIP

The Breeder

A good breeder houses the mother cat and her young in his or her home, rather than in the cattery. That's the only way the young ones learn to trust humans. They also stay with the mother until at least twelve weeks old. They have had their vaccinations. As the buyer, you should confirm the sale with a written purchase agreement. When you take possession of the kitten, get the vaccination record and the pedigree. The latter contains the names and colors of the ancestors for at least four generations, and usually any awards won by the parents. It should be issued by a recognized association, or you may encounter difficulties later on when you wish to show your animal.

This Persian kitten loves to stretch its legs after a nap in the hammock.

A Cat Bed

Cats like to be comfortable, so a basket with a cushion or a blanket is recommended. They love to curl up on the sofa or an armchair, on the windowsill, the heater, or a shelf, but they love a bed best of all.

Climbing Trees and Scratching Posts

In order to sharpen their claws, cats need an appropriate type of furniture; otherwise, they'll scratch up *your* living room furniture.

Scratching tree: Usually this takes on the function of a tree meant for climbing and living in. The trunk is wrapped with sisal; various elevated perches and hollows for cuddling invite cats to climb, sit, and hang out. (Pet stores have a broad selection to choose from.) A scratching tree is usually free-standing.

Scratching boards: These are covered with rough sisal and are affixed high enough on the wall, furniture, or door frame for the cat to stand up straight when it scratches.

Note: A light scratching rug or one of pasteboard may look like bargains, but they're not worth it; they'll be ripped to shreds in two shakes of a cat's tail. If you want to save money, glue some carpet remnants onto empty laundry detergent jugs that have been carefully washed. Cats can also play with them.

Litterbox

✔ Plastic tubs with an attached rim keep litter from flying out when the cat is pawing around.
✔ Litterboxes with drawers hold back odors and keep cats from urinating over the edge.
✔ There are cat toilets that automatically remove used litter and regularly supply fresh litter or neutralize odors electrically.

Cat litter: This is absorbent, odor-inhibiting, and guaranteed asbestos-free. Pet stores sell environment-friendly litter that can be disposed of with the household garbage. It is economical to use, since droppings clump together and can be easily removed.

Food and Water Dishes

Every cat needs one or two secure food dishes (for dry and canned food) and a water bowl.

Cat Grass

Cats like to nibble on grass, probably to help them regurgitate the hair they swallow when they groom themselves. Get them used to the grass designed for their use that's available in pet stores, since many plants in the home are poisonous to them (see Behavior Problems, page 30).

Purchase a cat grass kit from your pet store. The kit has grass seeds ready to sprout in a plastic tray. Add water, place the tray in a sunny spot, and in a few days you'll have cat grass. Also, add a bit of chopped parsley to your cat's food occasionally to satisfy its craving for green plants, and give it a little catnip to nibble on.

Checklist
Accessories

1 A wicker basket or a soft den for sleeping.

2 A litterbox with an attached rim and a drawer.

3 Cat litter, odor-inhibiting and guaranteed free of asbestos.

4 A scratching tree for climbing, playing, and sleeping, or a scratching board.

5 Comb and brush for grooming long-haired cats.

6 Food and water dish, sturdy and stable.

7 Cat grass, helpful in regurgitating the hair cats swallow when they groom themselves.

8 Toys, such as a plush mouse, all kinds of balls, cat lures—empty film containers filled with dried beans—and many more, available in pet stores and supermarkets.

The Trip Home

The kitten should be at least 12 weeks old before you take it home. Carry it in a basket or a plastic travel crate. If two people go to pick up the cat, the passenger can comfort the animal by talking to it. When you get home, place the crate on the floor and open the door.

Helping the Kitten to Adjust

✔ At first the kitten should get to know only one room and feel at ease in it. Provide a small dish of the food it's accustomed to (check with the previous owner), a dish with water, and the litterbox, which it will surely visit before long.

✔ Squat down by the basket and lure the kitten by softly calling the name you have chosen. It probably will meow pitifully. Answer it softly so it gets used to your voice.

✔ As soon as the kitten emerges from the basket, it's over its initial timidity. It probably will creep slowly and carefully on its belly and hide under the sofa or a cabinet, but that's normal feline behavior in unfamiliar surroundings. Keep small children and other house pets away for the time being.

✔ In the first hours and days, you shouldn't leave the kitten alone any more than necessary, since you have to make up for the loss of mother and siblings. Pet it, play with it, and cuddle with it; that will quickly strengthen its trust and its bonding with you.

Note: Remember that the kitten is always under foot; it runs between your feet, climbs up on you, and has no idea that closing doors can be life-threatening. So move carefully. Also, a kitten's urge to explore can get it into some of the most impossible circumstances, and, as a result, you have to keep a sharp eye out at all times.

The Older Cat

An older cat has already been used to its previous home, so it will take it longer to settle down; therefore, be prepared to exercise lots of patience.

A fearful cat: If it simply wants to hide, you'll have to put your expectations for an affectionate, cuddly house-mate on hold for a while. Try to figure out what frightens it. It may be specific movements or noises. Perhaps the cat previously lived with someone quiet, and maybe there's more commotion in your house. In order to win

Two older cats sniff and lick the little stranger in greeting and establish friendly contact.

The litterbox must be located in a place where the kitten doesn't feel that it's being watched.

Kittens like to contemplate new surroundings at leisure and from a comfortable place.

its trust, the same person should at first always be with it, feed it, and give it treats. Use no force, avoid coming upon the cat suddenly, and never corner it. Little by little, it will become less timid.

The problem cat: If you got the cat from an animal shelter, you may have taken on a problem; for example, it may reject its scratching post and scratch and bite you when you try to bring it to the post. The only solution is love and patience, and maybe a couple of tricks (see page 24). Refrain from grabbing it, feed it regularly, and act calm and composed. Eventually, it will gain more confidence.

Note: Sometimes homeopathic cures can help. Consult a veterinarian who has experience with them.

In the Yard

✔ Let your cat outdoors in a safely enclosed area only when it has become completely comfortable in the house. To be sure your cat

is safe, train it to walk on a leash attached to a harness.

✔ Stay close to the cat while it creeps carefully on its belly and sniffs each blade of grass and every pebble.

✔ Be sure that the cat can retreat if it is frightened by something. Usually it will retreat to a place where it already feels at ease (see Cats in the Yard, page 26).

Note: You should keep the cat indoors at all times unless you can be with it, to prevent injury or death by automobile or predator, or an unwanted pregnancy if the cat has not yet been spayed.

What Cats Like

✔ A favorite spot that no one competes for
✔ Long naps
✔ Being stroked, petted, and carried
✔ Snuggling and purring on their owner's lap
✔ Gentle brushing, but only when they're in the mood
✔ Lying and snoozing in the sun
✔ A clean litterbox
✔ Sharpening their claws anywhere they please
✔ Occasional playtime with people or another cat

Just a minute before, the kitten was scrambling on its climbing tree; from one moment to the next, it may fall asleep.

Many cats act as if they think that people were created to provide for their comfort. Like royalty presiding over their kingdom, they behave with persistence and tenacity until they get people to do what they want.

Housebreaking

For the most part, you can count on cats to use their toilet and to bury their leavings; even small kittens are usually already housebroken. Starting at about three weeks old, they begin to use the litterbox; they have observed their mother and imitated her actions. Help your kitten in the early days in your home to get used to the new place; housebreaking is usually accomplished right away. Also note the following:

Location: The litterbox should be in a quiet, protected place, such as in the bathroom.

Cleanliness: Fill the box with cat litter to a depth of 1½ to 2 inches (2 to 4 cm). Remove droppings and wet litter daily with a little shovel. Empty the litter once a week, clean the box with plain warm water, and refill it with fresh litter.

Note: Two cats stimulate one another to more frequent visits to the litterbox, since one wants to mark over the other. Either change the litter more often or make a second litterbox available.

Children like cats because they can cuddle and play with them.

If a Cat Is Not Housebroken

If the cat doesn't use its litterbox, but leaves souvenirs all around the house or apartment, there may be several reasons:

✔ The problem may be the litterbox. Maybe you're not cleaning it often enough, or the cat doesn't like the location.

✔ The cat is feeling amorous. Males and females spray everywhere in order to attract mates. Neutering is the only remedy.

✔ The cat is sick. If it is elderly, it might be incontinent. Take it to the veterinarian.

✔ The cat has a behavior disorder. The cause is often hard to determine. Consult a cat specialist or a book on cat behavioral problems.

✔ The cat is upset. New furniture, workmen in the house, or the presence of another cat may disturb its familiar surroundings. Give it lots of attention to strengthen its self-confidence, and, at the same time, try to break it from using the same area; for example, after cleaning it up, cover it with foil and spray it with mint or lemon oil, scents that cats don't like. Scolding or hitting are of no use.

Note: Use no cleaning agents that contain ammonia. They contain scents that remind cats of urine and stimulate them to leave their own scent again.

The Need to Scratch

Cats need a chance to scratch, even when they are free to roam outdoors, and for several reasons. They scratch to sharpen their claws, exercise the mechanism that extends and retracts the claws, show weaker cats their superiority, get rid of frustration and anger, and mark territory. Something to scratch on is important to have on hand, or the cat will go after your furnishings (see page 18).

Location of scratching post: Place it in a spot that the cat passes on its morning walk to the places where it grooms itself or eats. While it's scratching, it renews its markings with the scent glands on the forepaws, especially if it lives with another cat whose marking must be covered.

Training: As soon as you see that the cat is getting ready to scratch on an armchair or a rug, bring it to the scratching post. Gently place its paws on it and move them back and forth. Repeat the process a few times until the cat has gotten the idea.

The Scratching Post

The wrong location: Since the cat doesn't pass the post on its way through the living area, it has chosen a different spot to scratch. Move the mistreated piece of furniture and put the scratching post in its place.

Time: If you put up the scratching post after the cat had already gotten used to the wrong behavior, you now have to try to change its habits gently.

Scent marking: The cat scratches on your easy chair because it wants to mark over your scent and at the same time express its devotion. Sometimes it helps if you hang an old T-shirt over the rejected scratching post.

With a hearty yawn the cat lets the world know that it's ready for a nap.

Indoor Cats

A cat that has never run free will not feel hemmed in if it's kept indoors. The main thing is that it be as free and unhindered in its movement as it would be in the wild. As long as there are several places to take a walk, nooks and crannies to retreat to, observation points on windowsills or balconies, playthings to keep it busy, and care and attention from its human, the cat will lead a long and happy life. Usually, its behavior will be about the same as if it had more freedom.

The "first-class home," an expression of behavioral science, is extremely important for a cat. It may choose an entire room or just a preferred spot such as the sofa, the cupboard, or a warm windowsill. It likes to keep it all to itself, but it may also admit a partner.

The "second-class home" is an area the cat regards as its territory. It roams through it many

Dangers to Cats

Danger	Reason	How to Avoid the Danger
Balconies and open windows	Danger of falling	Secure with wire or nylon webbing.
Tip-out windows	Cat can get caught and strangle when it tries to jump through opening	Secure with special devices.
Hollow areas such as drawers or the drum of a washing machine	All dark hollows magically attract cats, and they can quickly get stuck in the trap, get shut in, or suffocate.	Check before closing drawers and cupboard doors, or before turning on appliances. Cover empty vases and toilets.
Doors that the cat can open if it jumps up and grabs the door handle	If the cat opens an outside door, you could have some unpleasant consequences.	Replace the door handle with a knob, or always lock the door.
Hot plates, open pots and pans with hot contents, chafing dishes, irons, candles, and burning cigarettes	Curious cats can be seriously burned.	Before leaving the kitchen, cover pots and pans; place a covered pot of water on a platter that is still hot from the oven; unplug irons; extinguish candles; avoid leaving burning cigarettes lying around.
Sewing needles and pins	Cats can step on them or swallow them.	Don't leave anything of this type around.
Cleaning and washing agents, chemicals, pills	Poisoning	Everything that's dangerous for children is also dangerous for cats. Keep such things locked up.
Plants such as cyclamen, azalea, ivy, hyacinth, philodendron, cowslip, poinsettia, dieffenbachia, and others	Poisoning	Usually, cats' instincts keep them from nibbling on poisonous plants; inexperienced cats should be denied access.

times throughout the day. If it lives with another cat, there must be enough room for them both to go their separate ways (see Helping a Cat to Become Used to Another Cat, page 27).

Cats and Balconies

A balcony or a roof terrace is fine for an indoor cat, since this enlargement of its territory offers it more variety in life, but you must be attentive to the following:
✔ The cat must always have a choice between sun and shade and be able to get back into the house or apartment.
✔ Secure the balcony or roof terrace with wire mesh so that the cat can't fall or stroll across the roof into someone else's apartment. Some landlords object to barriers, so it's best to clarify that beforehand.

Many cats prefer to lap water from a puddle rather than from their water bowl.

✔ Provide climbing opportunities and lookouts between windowboxes.
Note: Remember the dish with cat grass so that the cat doesn't misappropriate your plants (see Dangers to Cats, page 25).

Cats in the Yard

For your cat's safety and your peace of mind, it's best to keep your pet indoors. However, if you let your cat go outdoors, the following requirements should be met:
✔ Fence in your yard so that it's cat-proof; that will also keep out dogs. A fence about 6 feet (1.8 m) high is usually adequate.

✔ So that the cat can come and go at will, it's a good idea to install a cat door. You can get one at a pet store and install it yourself.

Tattooing

Tattooing can save the life of a cat that has run away or been stolen for laboratory research. Most animal research organizations have pledged to return or immediately report tattooed animals. Tattooing is done by the veterinarian on the inside of the thigh when the animal is under sedation, ideally when it's being neutered. The code is easy to decipher. It should include location, year, veterinarian, and serial number.

These protective measures are completed by recording the data in a registry.

Cat Meets Cat

It's possible to get an old and established cat used to a new one as long as you are patient and sensitive. Like a king in his realm, where people are tolerated, one cat regards a strange one as a rival and may fight it.

✔ Two young animals learn to get along best. After a couple of skirmishes, they'll like each other, play and cuddle together, and help each other pass the time.

✔ An older cat eventually gets used to a kitten. In your enthusiasm for the new arrival you must not neglect the older cat, or it will react by behaving badly; it may, for example, refuse to eat, or urinate right on the carpet (see If a Cat Is Not Housebroken, page 23). Also, pet it just as much as before, and if necessary, keep food dishes apart and provide a separate litterbox.

✔ You have to give two older cats plenty of room so that they can get out of each other's way. Divide your affection equally, but don't be disappointed if the two cats remain aloof from one another for life.

Checklist
Cats in the Yard

1 Keep cat away from roads.

2 Keep cat away from hunting areas; a hunter might shoot a cat by mistake.

3 Have all cats neutered, then they're more content to stay at home and not wander.

4 Provide a cat door for unrestricted coming and going into a secure yard or enclosed run.

5 Be sure the area is clean of animal feces that might harbor harmful organisms.

6 Establish regular mealtimes so that the cat comes inside punctually.

7 Have the cat tattooed.

8 Watch the cat while it is outside.

TIP

Cats and Children

Since cats like their rest and object to being handled roughly, a cat is not a good choice for small children up to the age of three years.

A cat can be entrusted to an older child, provided that you make sure that the animal is well cared for and fed. Show your child how to pick up and carry the cat properly, how to pet it—with the lay of the hair—and what kinds of play it likes. Also, explain to the child that it's always the cat that decides when it's in the mood for contact; otherwise there may be some painful misunderstandings. Children should be taught to respect a cat's special personality.

Cats and Other Pets

If the cat is the newcomer, it will have to adjust to the other animals. If it already rules in your household, in principle the same things must be observed that were described in the preceding paragraph. In order to avoid open conflict, you must be aware of the various behavior patterns of the individual animals.

Dogs: It's fairly common to see friendships between dogs and cats, but if they simply can't stand each other,

The kitten has trustingly snuggled up to its canine friend.

there's nothing you can do. Or perhaps the problem is lack of communication, since cats and dogs speak different languages. Whereas tail wagging in a dog is a friendly gesture, with a cat it expresses tension and nervousness. Rushing up to a cat is interpreted as an attack, and it raises a paw in defense; for a dog, on the other hand, it's an invitation to play.

It's good for a dog and cat to grow up together. Even an older dog that is well trained and devoted to its owner can learn to accept a cat. Teach it that, from now on, the cat is part of the pack. That can take a while, and until it happens, you shouldn't leave the two unsupervised. Trouble can result if a young dog is confronted by a self-assured cat. The cat can dominate the dog to the point that it becomes a fearful, unhappy animal that continually slinks away.

Rabbits, rodents, and small birds: These are potential prey for a cat and must be kept in secure cages. Also, the cat must not be left alone with them.

Traveling with a Cat

Before the trip: In preparation for a long trip, you should give the cat nothing to eat the night before and during the ride. The excitement of traveling affects a cat's

digestion in different ways. Many cats need to go to the litterbox right away; others react more calmly.

During the trip: Let the cat out of its travel crate only if it stays quietly on its seat. Be careful when opening doors and windows, and always use a cat leash to exercise the cat. Provide a litterbox and a water dish, even if the cat drinks little. Avoid drafts and direct sun. If you cross any international borders, have all necessary information about vaccinations together well in advance (from pet store owner, veterinarian, or clinic).

Airline travel: On scheduled flights cats can travel in the cabin in their travel crate. Check first with the airline.

Cats have no need for sweets in their diet.

Riding in the Car

Cats that don't like to ride in the car probably had something frighten them on their first exposure to it. Try to undo that by gradually getting the cat used to the car. At first, simply carry the cat in its travel case and place it into the car. Speak reassuringly to it, then bring it back inside. The next time, go for a short drive, and if the cat survives the stress, most of the difficulties are over.

If your cat cries and howls to get out of the crate, try to ignore it. A loose cat in the car is an invitation to disaster.

WHEN YOU GO ON VACATION

Leaving the Cat Home: *Cats feel most comfortable in their home environment. Find a person who can come to feed it and empty the litterbox, and has time to cuddle and play with the cat. You can find cat sitters listed in the want-ad section of newspapers, but be sure to carefully check their references.*

Taking the Cat With You: *You can get your cat used to traveling but if you're traveling to many different spots or your trip is too long, it might be too great a strain on the cat.*

Boarding the Cat: *The least stressful for you and the cat is to entrust it to friends. If you plan to leave the cat in a cat kennel, carefully inspect it beforehand. Since separation from its home and humans is very upsetting for a cat, it becomes particularly vulnerable to illnesses, a good reason to be sure it has had all its vaccinations (see page 56).*

Behavior Problems

Cats that suddenly display different behavior are usually reacting to some change in their environment; only rarely is it caused by illness. Try to find out what's bothering the cat; often, it's easy to eliminate the cause.

The timid cat: Very probably the cat has had some unpleasant experiences with people and needs to learn that you are going to treat it well, so it falls to you to rebuild the cat's trust in humans. You'll need lots of patience and love to do that. Be gentle, and always allow the cat a way to retreat into a secure place. Feed the cat several times a day by hand. Crouch down, hold out the food, and speak gently to it. When the cat approaches you, make no sudden moves that might frighten it. When the cat rubs you with its head you can stroke it gently with one finger.

The aggressive cat: Perhaps this cat is jealous of a new person in your life. Have this person feed the cat and pet it so that they get used to one another. If you have a new baby in the house, don't neglect the cat. Anxiety can be another cause. Treat the cat calmly and gently.

Nibbling plants: Perhaps the cat is nibbling plants because it can't find any cat grass (see page 19). Place a container of it far away from your houseplants and get the cat used to it. If the cat is bored, provide some variety in its life and keep the cat away from your plants; some of them may be poisonous (see Dangers for Cats, page 25).

Sucking: Some cats never get over this infantile behavior. Evidently they like to suck on cloth, wool, and the skin and hair of their owners. If this bothers you, forbid it consistently. Push the cat away and say *"No!"* emphatically, but never shout, or your cat will stay away from you entirely.

Grooming

Regular grooming is important, since it's helpful in detecting possible symptoms of illness.

What Cats Do for Themselves

Cats spend a lot of time thoroughly washing their fur with their tongue; they sharpen their claws on scratching posts or tree trunks, and use their teeth to tear hunks of meat and to chew bones.

What People Have to Do for Them

✔ Short- and longhaired cats need to be brushed every day while they're shedding so that they don't swallow too much fur in grooming. Brushing the coat with a coarse grooming brush also provides a massage.
✔ Longhaired cats need to be combed and brushed every day or their hair will become too matted. Bathe only when the fur is very dirty.
✔ Indoor cats that don't use their claws enough need to have the points of their claws trimmed. You can get a special clipper in the pet store.

✔ Give the cat small bones to chew on or rawhide bones for the teeth. (Make sure, however, that the bones are not too small or the cat will choke on them.) Have the veterinarian remove any tartar.
✔ Wipe eyes and ears with paper tissue. Dark clumps in the ears and holding the head to the side are signs of ear mites that must be treated by the veterinarian.

Proper Nutrition

Our house cats are biologically suited to life in the wild where they find everything they need in their prey: mice, small rodents, birds, and insects. You need to provide balanced nutrition, which is fairly easy, given the ample choice of prepared foods that are available.

Commercial Foods

These contain all the elements that cats need for proper nutrition, such as protein, fat, carbohydrates, vitamins, and trace elements, all of which are suited to nutrition for predators. The most expensive food is not always the best.

If you travel with your cats, don't forget to bring along their own dishes.

In choosing a brand, check the contents label and be sure that the food is free of preservatives.

Moist food is complete nutrition packed in cans and available in all types of flavors. It consists of a mixture of meat, giblets, or various kinds of fish, plus plant protein, grains, minerals, vitamins, and water.

Dry food is highly concentrated complete nutrition from which almost the entire water content has been removed. It's the equivalent of two or three times as much moist food, and cats like to nibble it. It's important for cats to drink plenty of water when they eat this food.

Food You Prepare

From time to time, you might want to prepare food yourself for your cat. The most important thing is to provide balanced nutri-

The thick, medium-long fur of the Norwegian Forest Cat needs weekly care.

tion, and that's not as easy as it sounds. An excess or deficiency in essential nutrients would be harmful to the cat in the long run. Feeding only meat leads to deficiencies; feeding liver exclusively results in Vitamin A toxicity. Consulting a nutritional value chart is helpful (see Nutrition Guide, pages 34–35).

However, cat food manufacturers have worked for decades with top researchers to develop foods that meet the nutritional needs of all sorts of cats in all stages of life and health. When all the nutrition your cat needs comes in a can or bag, why make work for yourself?

Because they are carnivores, cats need protein from animal sources. Their nutritional requirements are unique among mammals. They cannot adapt safely to a vegetarian diet, and they cannot thrive solely on diets designed for humans, dogs, or other animals. Therefore, creating nutritionally complete meals for a cat is a task best left to pet food manufacturers. "Don't try this at home." Without the help of an expert, such as a veterinarian, the cat owner cannot guarantee an adequate mix of proteins, carbohydrates, fats, vitamins, minerals, and amino acids essential to the feline diet.

For example, taurine, an amino acid, is an essential ingredient found in commercial cat foods. If a cat's food is taurine-deficient, it could develop eye disorders or cardiomyopathy (heart muscle disease).

Other nutritional additives in cat foods include vitamin supplements such as A, D, E, and B-complex, and minerals such as calcium, phosphorus, magnesium, potassium, salt, iron, and zinc. The feline diet requires a delicate balance of these ingredients to maintain proper body functions and cell growth. Too much or too little of one or the other can be harmful.

Nonnutritional additives include federal Food and Drug Administration-approved artificial and natural preservatives that extend a product's shelf life.

If you feel the need to cook for your cat, prepare homemade treats, not full meals (see page 34).

Foods to Avoid

✔ Don't feed your cat dog food, or let it steal food from your dog's dish. Dog food does not

TIP

What Cats Drink

Water: This is the proper drink for cats. Usually they take in enough fluid with their food to satisfy their thirst, but cats should always have a bowl with fresh water available.

Milk contains lots of protein and calcium and is particularly important for nursing kittens; however, cats can get diarrhea from cow's milk because of the lactose (milk sugar). This disappears when milk sours; in addition to sour milk, kittens can also have yogurt and cottage cheese with no problems.

contain enough protein or taurine for a cat's nutritional needs.

✔ Table scraps are okay as occasional treats, but don't let them take the place of cat food specially formulated to maximize your pet's good health. Never feed your cat any scraps that you would not eat.

✔ Don't give your cat bones. They might lodge in the throat or splinter and puncture the gastrointestinal tract.

✔ Don't allow your cat to eat raw meat or fish, which can contain parasites and harmful bacteria. Raw liver can cause vitamin A toxicity.

✔ Chocolate is toxic to cats as well as to dogs.

✔ Alcohol, even in small amounts, can be lethal to your cat.

Rules for Feeding

1 Always feed your cat at the same time of day. Cats get used to regular feeding times.

2 Give fresh canned food at every meal. Don't mix in leftover food; rather, reduce the new serving by the appropriate amount.

3 Don't serve anything directly from the refrigerator.

4 Don't give in to begging between meals, even if the cat meows ever so pitifully.

5 Don't withhold food from overweight cats; rather, reduce their portions.

6 Wash the food dish at every meal with hot water only. Use no cleaning agents.

7 Dog food is not suited to cats for any length of time, since it contains much less protein than cat food.

8 Vegetarian fare will cause deficiencies, as cats are dependent on animal protein.

Practical Snack Tips

✔ Well-cooked meat from cow, calf, sheep, rabbit, and wild game sliced into cat-sized hunks.
✔ Organ meats such as heart, stomach, and liver must be well cooked or they act as a laxative.
✔ Feed only fish that is cooked and deboned, once per week.
✔ Grated carrots and apples, cooked rice, steamed spinach, and instant oatmeal can be given in small quantities.
✔ Twice a week give a cooked egg yolk; give no egg white, since it destroys the vitamin B in the food.

✔ For between-meals snacks, give a teaspoonful of cottage cheese or some grated, mild hard cheese two or three times a week, and cat vitamin flakes from the pet store as indicated on the label.

Diet for Fat Cats

Neutered cats often become sluggish and eat to pass the time. Overweight animals are more prone to sickness. Eliminate all between-meals snacks, cut down serving sizes to about half, or feed commercial diet foods. They are available as canned or dry food from the veterinarian or pet store. Be consistent even if the cat begs for more.

Don't starve fat cats; instead, cut their portions in half.

Diet for Mild Intestinal Problems

Prescription: Two teaspoons of cottage cheese and one teaspoon of mashed potatoes (prepared with water). After two to three days, replace cottage cheese with cooked meat or fish.

Dose: One heaping tablespoon freshly prepared five times a day. In addition, fresh water with a pinch of salt.

Duration: Have the cat fast for two days; then three to five days on the diet.

Cat Food Test

Does your cat's food meet these four criteria?
✔ It is nutritionally adequate.
✔ It supplies enough calories to meet its energy requirements.
✔ It contains the nutrients in a form—dry, semi-moist, or canned—that can be utilized by the cat.
✔ It tastes good!

A cat begs for food by rubbing its head, throat, and sides against its owner.

The Proper Daily Amount of Canned Food

Age or Weight	Meals	Amount per Day
Young cats up to 4 months	4	About 9 oz. (250 g)
Half-grown (4 to 7 months/ 4 pounds (1.5 kg)	3	Up to 12 oz. (350 g)
Adults 7 months or older; 7¾– 11 lbs. (3.5–5 kg)	2	4 to 7 oz. (150–200 g)
Senior (over 10 years)	3–4	4 to 5 oz. (120–150 g)
Pregnant cat	3–4	13 oz. (360 g)
Nursing cat	3–4	16 oz. (450 g)
Breeding male	2	14 oz. (400 g)

A cat crouches in front of the dish to eat and drink.

Feeding on Trips

When you take your cat on the road with you, pack enough of its regular food to last the entire trip. Pack a container of water from home. Changes in food or water can cause vomiting and diarrhea. Feed your cat a light meal about six hours before you start your trip, and give a few sips of water before leaving.

Breeding

The best advice on breeding cats is *don't do it!* There are far too many homeless cats that were once someone's cute little kittens. It has been calculated that in just five years, a single pair of cats that give birth to about fourteen kittens per year, in three litters can have 65,536 descendants! With such a host, it's sure that not all will find a good home for a long time. They wander around, become ill and under-nourished, get run over or shot, or end up in experimental labs. Large colonies of feral cats, malnourished and disease-ridden, are becoming a serious problem in all areas of the United States and Canada. The only reason to ever consider breeding is maintenance and improve-ment of a particular breed of cat. The responsi-ble breeder has found a home for every kitten before the queen is introduced to a male.

Neutering and Spaying

Neutering is an operation to remove the tes-ticles or the ovaries. A female cat can be spayed at a very early age; operations at an early age seem to have no effect on the growth or trainability of the cat. The operation is per-formed by a veterinarian while the animal is under general anesthetic.

Mating Behavior

When a female cat comes into heat, she leaves not the slightest doubt about her condi-tion. She is increasingly agitated for three to six days, scarcely eats, meows and howls, rubs against things, and continually wants to be petted. At the climax of this process, she cries out loudly and continually rolls around on the floor.

A male cat is ready to mate practically all year long. When he detects the scent of a female in heat, he sprays everywhere to leave his scent marking behind. He's on the move all night long and battles other male cats for the favor of a female.

At home, the two mates are presented to one another. If the female rejects the male, nothing can be done and another suitor must be found.

In the wild, the female seeks out the male. If she attracts a male by meowing, he courts her by cooing, running back and forth in front of her, and spraying enthusiastically.

Mating

A female that's ready to mate cowers, raises her hindquarters, cocks her tail to the side, and treads with her hind feet. When the male mounts her, he seizes her by the scruff of the neck; with a couple of pushes, he completes the mating, which the female accompanies with a loud cry. Immediately afterward he flees from the angry blows of her paws. There's a reason for the yelling and slapping: The penis is equipped with barbs that scratch the walls of the vagina when it is pulled out. This shock triggers ovulation, but the discomfort is quickly forgotten, for it

For three-day-old kittens the day consists mostly of drinking and sleeping.

usually stops when the mating is over. Since the female may afterwards mate with other males, she may give birth to kittens with a number of different sires.

At the age of eight weeks these Ragdolls are already on a discovery tour.

Breeding Purebred Cats

In order to breed purebred cats, you must be knowledgeable about heredity, and have time, space, and money. Also consider the following:

✔ The goal is to improve the breed, not simply to have kittens.

✔ The mother cat must be healthy (see Vaccinations, page 53) and exhibit the typical traits of her breed. She should not be bred before the age of one year, and no more than twice a year.

✔ The female cat is taken to the male. You can locate a recognized breeding male by consulting the official directory of certified breeding males of all breeds, produced by a purebred cat association (see Information, page 62).

✔ Stud fees can amount to well over $100, which doesn't include travel or shipping expenses in cases where the male cat is located far away.

✔ In choosing a male cat, try to create a balance between good and bad points relative to the breed standards. Consult an experienced breeder.

✔ Only by examining the offspring will you know if the male and female cats are a good match and produce young that conform to the breed standards.

Pregnancy and Birth

A veterinarian can palpate kittens at about 20 days into gestation. The teats, which usually are scarcely visible through the fur, become firm and pink and begin to stand up. Starting with the fifth week the belly becomes visibly rounder.

Food: Especially now, the cat needs nutritious food and lots of protein from a good premium-quality food.

The due date is calculated from the first mating plus 63 days. Variations of seven days either way are normal.

A queening box can be made by putting a thick layer of newspaper topped by a clean cloth on the bottom of a cardboard box that measures about 16 by 20 inches (40 × 50 cm), with walls about 1 foot high (30 cm). Put the box in a quiet place so the cat can get used to it.

Birth: You can tell when the cat is ready by her restlessness. She keeps jumping into the queening box, digging in the litterbox, and following you around. If you speak gently to her, she may lie quietly. Shortly before birthing begins she breaks water and the first little one is expelled in an amniotic sack. The mother rips it open with her teeth if it hasn't already burst, bites off the umbilical cord, and eats the afterbirth that appears after the next series of contractions, then she licks the newborn dry. One by one, the kittens are born the same way. That can last for an hour or two, and sometimes an entire day.

How Kittens Develop

One to seven days: Newborn kittens are blind and deaf, and have a downy coat of fur. They weigh between 2½ and 4½ ounces (70 to 130 g). The instinct to eat directs them immediately to the right place—the mother's teats. They grope their way to the teats, latch on to suck, and stimulate milk flow by kneading with their front paws. They are entirely dependent on the mother's care. If she trusts her owner, she may allow her little ones to be picked up, carefully stroked, and spoken to softly.

Eight to twelve days: Birth weight has doubled, eyes begin to open, kittens purr audibly when they suckle, and interest in the surroundings begins to increase.

The kitten becomes rigid as soon as the mother picks it up by the neck.

Thirteen to twenty days: Movements are already somewhat more determined, and kittens paw their siblings. Kittens begin to crawl and look curiously and wide-eyed over the edge of the box. They show no fear with people they know, but spit at strangers.

Twenty-one to twenty-five days: With the first steps outside the box, movements become gradually more purposeful. The kittens play awkwardly but actively with one another. The first milk teeth appear.

Three to four weeks: Time for the first solid food. Kittens use the litterbox for the first time. They learn by imitating the mother, who no longer concerns herself with their cleanliness. They are still timid with people, and especially with noise, commotion, and sudden movements. Their humans help them understand that petting and getting picked up mean warmth and security.

Five to six weeks: Kittens jump and climb out of the queening box. Chasing and catching siblings is the order of the day. The mother regularly brings in prey when she has a chance. She plays with the youngsters and teaches them the fine points of cat language: spitting, arching the back, and soothing and threatening gestures.

Seven to eight weeks: Kittens play and fight tirelessly, exercising their bodies. The bonding with the mother diminishes in intensity, but contact with her and with siblings remains very important. Even humans are invited to play, which builds trust.

Three to four months: The kittens are now so independent that they can move to a new home, but first they have to take a trip to the veterinarian for their vaccinations (see page 56).

Finding a Good Home

It's sad to part with those cute little kittens.

TIP

Orphan Kittens

It's no simple matter to nurse days-old kittens back to health. In the first two weeks, use a heating pad or heat lamp to provide the necessary warmth of about 80 to 90°F (25 to 30°C). Feed every two hours—even during the night—with a special milk bottle (available at the pet store), or, if the kitten is too weak to suckle, dribble in milk with an eyedropper or a disposable syringe with the needle removed. Then massage the abdomen to stimulate digestion. You can get special milk from the pet store or use twice the amount of baby formula prescribed for an infant. Cow's milk is not digestible because of its high lactose content.

But if you find a loving, permanent home for each of them, it's a little easier to say goodbye. Unless you are selling purebred kittens to a serious breeder, it's a good idea to have them neutered before placing them, or to obtain a written spay-neuter agreement from the buyer or adoptive owner. Ask the prospective owner these questions:

✔ Will you keep the kitten indoors?
✔ Have you had cats before?
✔ What did you feed them?
✔ Did they get proper veterinary care?
✔ What happened to them?
✔ Do you have other pets?

Only if each question is answered to your satisfaction should you place your precious kitten with its new owner.

UNDERSTANDING YOUR CAT

"You have to have the ear of a cat in order to distinguish the voice of an ant from that of a ladybug," according to a cat enthusiast. That's only a slight exaggeration, for a cat's senses are greatly in tune with its role as a hunter.

What Cats Can Do

Physique: The extreme suppleness of the cat's body enables it to move in a remarkable variety of ways. It curls up to sleep; when it wakes up, it stretches, lolls about, and arches its back. It slips nimbly through small spaces or squeezes itself flat as a pancake under a cupboard. And with dreamlike surefootedness it balances on top of a fence.

Limbs: From a standing position, a cat can jump five times its height. When stalking, it moves extremely slowly and with perfect control; although its acceleration is explosive, it can't maintain it for very long. With the help of its claws, it easily climbs an object, only to climb down head-first in a helpless slide. It's much more successful in coming down backwards.

Paws and tail: The pads of the paws allow the cat to tread noiselessly. There are four claws on the hind paws, and five on the front; they can be retracted into skin sheaths. The cat uses its tail to maintain its balance in falls and jumps.

While playing, the kitten learns to stand on its hind legs.

Sense Perception

Hearing: A cat's ears are big, movable funnels that can be focused on any sound independently of one another, and that can hear in a frequency range up to 65 kHz; a human's hearing is sensitive up to only 20 kHz.

Sight: Cats display night vision in subdued light, not total absence of light. In darkness the pupils become very large in order to collect maximum light; the more light there is, the smaller they become.

Touch: With the exceptional sensitivity of the whiskers, the sensor hairs over the eyes, and the hairs on the forelegs, cats can find their way even in the dark.

Smell and taste: These senses are closely connected in cats and enable them to broaden their sense perceptions.

Cat Body Language

Some people believe that arching the back is a sign of submissiveness, but that's one of many misunderstandings concerning cats; in their system of body language, arching signifies defensiveness and the order: "Leave me alone!"

Cats cultivate many more social contacts than humans realize. They communicate with a combination of body language and utterances. They express their feelings precisely and clearly through voice, posture, and movement. They use this behavior with people too. If you determine what your cat is trying to say, you will soon learn how to assess its mood.

How to Read a Cat's Moods

Well-being: The cat looks relaxed and friendly as it sits or lies around. The ears are forward and slightly turned out; the eyes look out peacefully and blink, according to the brightness. It runs to greet you with tail carried high and head raised. If it wants to snuggle, it closes its eyes and purrs as it rubs

Hide-and-seek is part of a kitten's daily training.

against your legs, or it rubs its head against your hand.

Alertness: The cat's wide-eyed, seemingly innocent look doesn't reveal that it's tense, but that can be detected by looking at the pointed ears and the tail that sweeps gently back and forth. Playfully it tries to reach whatever has stimulated its alertness.

Defense: If the cat doesn't want to be disturbed in its resting place, it first communicates restraint: The ears fold toward the sides, the pupils enlarge, and the whiskers lie back. Then the cat shows its claws and angrily deals a few blows with its paws. At

Lurking near the opening until the opponent drops its guard is part of the game.

The cat siblings play at attack and defense.

the same time it hisses and spits or growls deep in its throat and increases the pitch to a shrill cry according to its level of anger.

Fearful restraint: The cat tries to make itself inconspicuous. The ears turn to the side, and the face appears retracted, as does the entire body. As the fear increases, it quickly turns into defensiveness: The cat's hair stands on end, the ears are laid back toward the body, the pupils become enormous, the tail wags back and forth, and the cat squawks loudly.

Attack: A cat can show readiness to attack another cat, as when male cats fight and con-

test territory. Such a confrontation is signaled by staring at one another.

Playfulness: If a cat wants to play, it will roll over and expose the abdomen. During the breeding season, it also means the cat wants to mate.

Submission: A fearful or timid cat will crouch and slink along the floor, head and tail down, ears flat along its head. It might show this behavior if a stranger approaches. If it is threatened by a dominant cat or other animal, this is the cat's way of showing deference.

BODY LANGUAGE
OF CATS

If you want to learn cat language, you have to interpret your cat's behavior properly.

 This is what my cat does.

 What is my cat trying to tell me?

! *The correct response.*

Two cats wrestle with one another.

They are trying out fighting tactics they will need later on.

Don't butt in; these games are very important parts of their socialization.

The cat arches its back and raises its hair.

It is showing uncertainty and defensiveness.

You can speak reassuringly to it, but don't touch it.

The cat rolls around on the ground.

It feels content.

You can stroke its abdomen.

The cat is hissing with ears pointed back.

It is ready to attack.

Don't try to touch it, or it will lash out.

☞ The cat climbs a tree.

❓ It's looking for an elevated spot.

❗ If it doesn't come down by itself, you'll have to help it.

The cat hisses at ☞ the kitten.

It's reprimanding ❓ the youngster.

Don't meddle; ❗ pecking order is being reinforced.

☞ The male cat checks beneath the tail of the other cat.

❓ The raised tail is a sign of friendly greeting.

❗ Leave the two cats alone.

☞ One cat licks another behind the ears.

❓ The two like each other.

❗ You can pet them.

🖐 The cat crouches in waiting.

❓ It has some prey in its sights.

❗ Interfere only if it's hunting a bird or other prey you want to protect.

Means of Expression

Purring: With this sound young cats communicate to the mother that they are in good health. Once the cat is grown, cats still express themselves by purring, but the meaning changes according to the situation and social relationships. Mother cats purr when they groom themselves and when the little ones are suckling. Kittens purr when they want to invite adult cats or people to play. Superior animals purr when they want to approach an inferior peacefully. Sick and very weak cats purr to appease stronger cats.

Pawing: In order to stimulate milk flow, baby cats massage the mother's belly with their paws. Grown cats use this juvenile behavior to express their trust.

Licking: The mother cat licks its young and thereby stimulates excretion. A male cat licks a female it's courting. Licking is a friendly gesture that stems from the sex and care-giving drive. Sometimes a cat will quickly lick its fur while it's doing something else, a sign that it doesn't know what it should do, and it is performing a substitute behavior. That's also known as *displacement grooming.*

Rubbing: Your cat leaves its distinctive scent when it rubs against something. Glands along the lips, on the chin, and between the eye and ear secrete a scent undetectable to humans, but readily recognized by other cats. When a cat rubs against you, it is marking you as a favorite person. When it rubs against furniture, walls, doorways, and other pets, it is saying, "This is mine." Cats also rub each other in greeting, much as people kiss.

Spraying: A more emphatic method of claiming territory, spraying is executed by intact males and sometimes queens and neutered cats. The cat backs up to a tree, doorway, rock, or other object, lifts its tail, quivers, and sprays a stream of urine. The pungent scent is unmistakable to cats and humans alike.

Social Behavior

As a born individualist, the cat takes a backseat to no one, yet it cultivates social contact. It patrols certain paths through its territory that are used by other cats in the area, but usually not at the same time. If one cat encounters another on its excursions, it avoids crossing paths with it, but if that happens anyway, both remain apart from one another and wait until one of them decides to resume the journey, or they go off in opposite directions.

Congregations of Cats

In certain situations and social circumstances, cats live in clusters, as in the Colosseum in Rome or the cemeteries in Paris.

Just as unusual is the cat congregation. Male and female cats sit down peacefully and harmoniously at secret meeting places. Nothing more may happen, and after a few hours or an entire night, the congregation dissolves.

The cat marks the stone with special scent glands on its temples and the corners of its mouth.

Cat Language at a Glance

Body Language	Facial Expression	Vocalization	Meaning
Erect posture; head and tail held high	Ears slightly turned outward; eyes still	Meowing in greeting	Friendly contact
Sits with tail draped over paws	Ears as described above; eyes blinking		Calm and relaxed
Lying with front paws kneading your lap	Ears and eyes as described above	Purring	Contentment
Kneading with its front paws as it rubs against your legs; rubbing you with its head, holding its tail high		Meowing; purring	Begging for food and attention
Tense; tip of tail twitches	Ears pointed straight ahead; eyes big and round	Meowing	Alertness
Stiff legs; back slightly raised; hackles raised; lashing tail bent in a hook	Ears pointed backward; narrowed pupils	Growling, spitting; sustained rising and falling howl as a threat	Ready to attack, usually another cat
Rear legs slightly bent; head lowered; arched back; tail lashing back and forth	Ears folded to the side; pupils wide open	Hissing; spitting	Ready to fight; angry; ready to come to blows
Cowering; trying to become inconspicuous	Ears laid back; half-closed eyes; face somewhat turned aside		Fearful restraint
Hackles raised; tail lashing back and forth	Ears laid back on head; enlarged pupils	Squawking	Fear turns into defensiveness

10 Golden Rules
for Training Cats

1 You can train a kitten that has learned by imitating its mother only if you act as an example for it.

2 If the cat is older, you must teach it to avoid anything that leads it into temptation or that doesn't agree with it.

3 Always speak softly to the cat; it will do what you want only when it trusts you.

4 If something is forbidden once, it must remain so; for example, keep the cat from jumping up on the table at all times, not only when it's set for your meal.

5 Praise and pet the cat lovingly if it obeys.

6 Scold in an abrupt voice, and always with the same words, such as "Yuck!," "No!," "Down!," or "Get out!"

7 Don't yell at the cat, and never call it by name as you reprimand it.

8 Proceed with iron-clad consistency. Be sure other family members follow the same cat training rules.

9 Never hit the cat! It would not understand, and would only learn to fear your hand.

10 If you catch the cat red-handed, you can administer a dose of fright. An unwelcome stream of water from a squirt bottle, or the clattering of a small chain are very unpleasant to cats and break them of the bad habit.

There is an interesting brotherhood of male cats, according to behavior specialist Paul Leyhausen, who describes the formal pecking order that arises among male cats in a particular area. Young male cats enjoy a grace period in this brotherhood up to a certain age. They are taken in, occasionally properly put in their place, but involved in no battles, as if they were being given time to adjust to the rigors of cat life.

Keeping Your Cat Busy

Kittens have tremendous energy for playing. Since mother and siblings are no longer around, you now fill the role.

The Need to Play

When they are only one month old, kittens begin to explore their surroundings. They can hardly hold themselves up on their legs, but their thirst for action is unquenchable. The playfulness that's so amusing to us is nothing but a rehearsal of all the types of behavior that the kitten will need in its later life. In social play the siblings learn how to get along with one another; in the various games of pursuit and combat, they test the behavior they will later use with other cats. The threatening body language with which they try to intimidate each other is all in fun, but the facial expressions and gestures are unambiguous. With hackles raised and a masterfully arched back, they present their broad side; ears are laid back and their gaze transfixes their adversary. Hissing, spitting, biting, and scratching are part of the program, as is the final frantic chase.

The hunting instinct awakens around the end of the sixth week of life. Then, stalking, lurking, hunting, and jumping are practiced tirelessly. A kitten will turn into a healthy animal only if it has an opportunity to develop its physical abilities every day.

"I can jump even higher," the cat that is watching seems to be thinking.

What Cat Play Means for Humans

If a kitten can accumulate positive experiences with people during this important socialization phase, it will join into a real partnership with its new owners and try to use up in your home the energy it formerly worked off with mother and siblings. Provide a wide choice of toys and lots of time. Perhaps as an adult the kitten will retain its youthful disposition and enjoy playing to an advanced age.

Cats have a mind of their own. Even if you're in the mood for playing, your cat will decide when it's ready—usually toward evening, when cats are inclined to become spunky.

Some Little Tricks

Capitalize on the natural abilities of cats, such as balancing and jumping. Naturally, there has to be a stimulus for the cat to do precisely what you want. Tempt the cat with a treat and always use the same command ("*Come on!*"). If it negotiates a broomstick balanced between chairs, praise and reward it with a treat, then remove the broomstick and get your cat to jump from chair to chair. When it's mastered the trick, it will repeat it without enticement, merely upon command—but only as long as it's having fun. You can't force a cat to do anything.

Note: Be sure the broom is secured on both ends or the cat will never venture onto it again.

Cats can amuse themselves for hours by watching something moving under a blanket

Hiding

Cats like to hide in hollows. Make all kinds of hiding places available, such as a newspaper that you set up like a roof and rattle a bit, or a blanket under which something mysterious is moving. Everything means "There's a mouse in the house!" and they become fascinated.

Even an empty cardboard box is a favorite hiding place, and if the opening is very small, the cat won't rest until it's squeezed through and can rustle around inside. It's even better if you can act like a second cat that wants to go after it. The first cat will defend its spot with fang and claw, so don't offer your hand as a plaything, or you'll pick up some painful scratches (see Important Note, page 63).

Playing Ball

Chasing a ball, catching it, rolling it daintily with the paws, and pouncing on it with its entire body is one of a kitten's favorite activities.

Give it a hard rubber ball with a surface that's not too slick as soft rubber balls are too easy to bite and swallow.

Pawing, catching, and releasing the toy, then starting all over again.

Searching for Treats

Cats learn surprisingly quickly by observing. Once they have seen where their treats come from, they'll try to get into the container themselves. This natural impulse to get food for themselves can be converted into an exciting game: Hide the treat in a box; if the cover fits fairly tightly, the cat will scratch, pry, and gnaw until it gets in and can help

A closed box is no problem for a cat. It merely does what you have demonstrated for it dozens of times.

itself. Your cat might repeat this clever trick with your garbage can, the container of delicious table scraps. Be sure the receptacle has a tightly fitting cat-proof cover or is secure behind a well-latched cabinet door.

Stalking and Chasing

Crouch and clap your hands on the floor. When the cat slips out of the room, pretend to stalk after it. The cat will be waiting for you until you steal around the corner, then it storms off, so you hide. After a minute it will come to see what's keeping you, and everything starts all over. This is the same way you play with children, but then, cats are a lot like kids.

Jumping Up

Maybe your cat is a gifted jumper. Many can be inspired to do flips. You can easily make the prop used for that: Attach a feather to a rubber band and dangle it in front of the cat's nose. It will try to paw it, jump after it, and catch it.

Coming when Called

It doesn't take long for a cat to associate the sound of the can opener with dinner. So from the beginning call the cat as you open the can. Call its name at other times during the day, and when it runs up to you, reward it with a treat. In a few weeks it should respond when you call its name.

"I'm higher than you are" provides endless fun for cats.

HEALTH CARE FOR YOUR CAT

It is said that cats have nine lives. Their ability to bounce back after a serious illness is often astonishing, but be sure your cat has its vaccinations so it's fully protected.

Vaccinations

Inoculations are the most important and most valuable preventive health measures for your cat. In order to be vaccinated, the animal must be healthy and free of parasites. Ask your veterinarian to do a stool analysis before giving the vaccinations. The veterinarian records the vaccinations and indicates when certain ones need to be repeated (see Vaccination Schedule, page 56). The vaccination program for cats covers the following illnesses:

Panleukopenia: This highly contagious viral infection is transmitted not only from animal to animal but also by intermediary means, including even hands, shoes, and other objects.

Feline respiratory diseases: This is the most widespread of illnesses, especially in young cats. Vaccinated cats can also become ill, but not as seriously as those not vaccinated.

Feline leukemia: This is transmitted from cat to cat (by biting, licking, and mating). Detectable by a test performed by a veterinarian.

Immunizations are a must for keeping young cats healthy.

Rabies: Communicable to humans (see page 54). The immunization is a prerequisite for travel abroad and for cat shows.

Feline Infectious Peritonitis (FIP): The FIP blood test and FIP immunization are very controversial. Get advice from several veterinarians.

Note: The feline immunodeficiency virus (FIV) belongs to the same viral group as the AIDS pathogen in humans, but it is not a threat to humans. Therefore, if your cat is ill with FIV, there's no need for you to get rid of it. Get advice from a veterinarian.

Worming

Young kittens are first wormed at the age of two weeks. Too frequently, worm medicines harm the intestinal membranes of kittens; therefore, you should bring a stool specimen to the veterinarian every four weeks until the cat is six months old, then you should administer worm medicine only if worms are present. That also makes it possible to determine the type of worms. Don't use any so-called comprehensive worm medicines, as they are too strong.

A preventive worm treatment is adequate about every six months to counteract roundworms and hookworms.

Note: With indoor cats, which usually don't become reinfested, worming need not be repeated.

Communicable Diseases

An indoor cat that has been immunized and that eats only cooked or commercial food rarely picks up pathogens that are also dangerous to humans, with some important exceptions:

Rabies: Every cat that runs free must be immunized against rabies. You need to have an indoor cat immunized if you plan to take the cat on an international trip. Since the requirements vary from country to country, find out what you need to know well in advance by consulting a veterinarian, or the consulate of the country you are planning to visit.

Toxoplasmosis: This is a danger to pregnant women, since the unborn child can suffer severe damage to brain and eyes if the mother is exposed. At the beginning of pregnancy, therefore, women should notify their doctors that they own a cat and have it examined for toxoplasmosis twice in the space of six weeks.

Note: For the duration of the pregnancy, the woman should not get too physically close to the cat, and someone else should clean out the litterbox. There is no reason to get rid of the cat.

Microsporosis: This is caused by a skin fungus and manifests itself in hair loss and itching. You must consult a veterinarian for treatment. In order to prevent reinfection, disinfect everything that the cat has come into contact with. Wash your hands after touching the cat.

Roundworms and tapeworms: Preventive worming is effective in preventing incidence of these worms.

Grooming is a sure sign that the cat is healthy and content.

Fleas and ticks: There are preparations, drops, powders, and shampoos that can be used against fleas. Remove ticks with tweezers, and drop them in a jar of alcohol to kill them.

First Aid

You can treat minor health problems yourself with natural medicines. If the problems persist longer than two days, you must take the cat to the veterinarian.

✔ In the case of diarrhea, discontinue any food that may be causing problems, such as milk, raw liver, or spoiled meat. Administer chamomile or peppermint tea with crushed blueberries (see Treat Illness, pages 58–59).

✔ For constipation, add a little milk or one to two teaspoonfuls of olive oil to the food.

✔ For colds: consult your veterinarian.

Recognizing Health Problems

Symptoms	Possible Causes That You Can Treat	When to Seek Veterinary Help
The cat has no energy	Boredom; no stimulus to play; refuses food	Vomiting; diarrhea
Vomiting	Eating grass; hair ingested while grooming; food too cold	Apathy; diarrhea
Salivating	Strong excitement; possible illness	Eats very little
Bad breath	Strong-smelling food, such as fish	Vomiting; trembling; salivating
Continual thirst	Spicy food	Weight loss; vomiting
Diarrhea	Improper food	Bloody stool; vomiting
Overeating	Eating too quickly after being outside	Clay-colored droppings; unkempt fur; emaciation
Straining without eliminating feces or urine	Lack of exercise; improper food	Cries of pain
Runny eyes	Drafts; irritating cleaning agents	Purulent discharge
Sneezing, coughing	Drafts; rapid change from hot to cold	Fever; labored breathing; expulsion of phlegm
Scratching	Cleaning fur; fleas	Continual scratching everywhere
Prolapsed third eyelid	Closes it when it's uncomfortable because of infection or foreign object in eye	Discharge from eye
Shaking or holding head at an angle		Scratches behind ear; earache
Bleeding	Small cuts	Blood from mouth, anus, genitals, or large wounds

Vaccination Schedule for Health Maintenance

	Age	Panleukemia	Respiratory Illness	Feline Leukemia	Rabies
Basic Immuni-zation	5 weeks	●	●		
	12 weeks	●	●	●	●
	4 months	●	●	●	●
	after one year	●	●	●	●
	after two years	●	●	●	●**
	after three years	●	●	●*	●
	after four years	●	●		●

Note: Until recently there has not been a vaccination for FIP (see page 53). Since its use is currently very controversial, you should consult several veterinarians.
*Important: The most recent discoveries concerning feline leukemia immunizations indicate that a lifelong immunity is in place for the cat starting at the age of four years. Immunizations beyond that point are not required.
**Rabies schedule varies from state to state.

✔ For cough lasting longer than 12 hours, consult your veterinarian.
✔ For bruises, apply dressings of tincture of arnica or calendula (stick to recommended concentration), and one to three times a day give one arnica-D3 tablet.
✔ Treat superficial injuries with a dressing of tincture or salve of calendula, or a tincture of camomile. Follow that with tablets as with the treatment for bruises. Herbal remedies are not always effective, however. If you don't notice improvement within 48 hours, take your cat to the veterinarian.
✔ After an accident, lay the cat on its side on a blanket, cover it, and make a bed for it in a basket or on your lap. Keep the head slightly down so that blood gets to the brain. Get the cat to the veterinarian as quickly as possible, after calling ahead to say that you're coming.

It's a warning sign if a kitten loses interest in its toy.

The Aging Cat

You have spent many happy years with your cat; now it has grown old, it is not as limber, and it prefers a soft cushion that it can take over in comfort. It eats less and has gotten thinner. Also, it grooms less frequently and has a rough coat. When the cat gets older, don't change anything you don't have to in its surroundings. Any excitement, such as a young kitten, would be as stressful as a move to a different house.

Care: Even if you detect no problems, you should have your aging cat checked by the veterinarian every three to four months. It may suffer from constipation, dental problems, or difficulty hearing and seeing. The main thing is to continue to act lovingly with the animal.

On its expeditions through its territory, the cat gracefully overcomes all obstacles.

Euthanasia: When the cat gets sick and can no longer live without pain, you should consult with the veterinarian to see if euthanasia is the best solution. Only the veterinarian is in a position to administer an injection that will gently put the animal to sleep. If you hold the cat in your arms until the end, and stroke it and talk with it, it will not experience any fear or pain. Find out also if you can bury your animal in your own yard. The veterinarian can help you with the disposal of the mortal remains; sometimes there are regulations concerning the disposal of deceased pets.

The Veterinarian

Since you already have to visit the veterinarian at least once a year for vaccinations, you should look for an expert who knows cats well. Ask for recommendations from other cat owners, the pet store, or a cat breeders' association.

✔ Transport the cat in its travel cage or kennel; don't let it out in the waiting room.

✔ Give the veterinarian a short but precise description of the symptoms, and answer his or her questions precisely. If necessary, bring a stool sample.

✔ If medication is prescribed, stick to the dosages and time limits. Follow precisely all orders from the veterinarian.

A sick cat is listless, stops eating, and may continually scratch itself. Further indications of illness include continuous thirst, diarrhea, frequent vomiting, fever, coughing, and extreme emaciation. In such cases you must not delay taking the cat to the veterinarian.

Caring for the Cat

Sick bed: Put a cushion into a shallow cardboard box or a basket with a slightly raised edge so the cat can't fall out. Cover the box or basket with a cloth that can be washed.

Location: Keep the cat in a warm, draft-free place. If other cats are present, isolate the sick one if it has a contagious disease.

Feeding: Feed with fresh, warmed treats or tasty nutritional concentrates available

Pad the sickbed with a cushion.

from the veterinarian. If the cat has difficulty chewing, puree the chunks of food, or dribble lightly salted beef or chicken broth into the side of its mouth by using a syringe with no needle. Proceed slowly so the cat doesn't choke.

Drinking: Fresh water must always be available. If the sick cat doesn't drink enough, dribble water into the cat's mouth.

Taking the Cat's Temperature

This is best done by two people. One holds the cat securely by the shoulders and forefeet and talks quietly to it, while the other lifts the tail and inserts the lubricated digital thermometer into the rectum as horizontally as possible only as far as a little less than 1 inch (2 cm). The normal temperature is between 100° and 102.5°F (37.8° and 39.2°C).

Injections: A cat that suffers from diabetes must have an injection every day. The veterinarian will show you how it's done.

Note: If the sick cat tries to defend itself with its claws, wrap it up in a big towel to avoid getting scratched.

Applying an ointment or eyedrops to the upper eyelid.

When you administer eardrops, gently pull the ear out of the way.

Drops: Dribble them on the cat's paw; it may lick them off, at least if they don't have a bad taste. Bitter medicines can be given as described in the section on feeding (facing page).

Treating the Eyes and Ears

Eye ointments: Grasp the cat's head firmly from behind and simultaneously pull back the upper eyelid with the index finger. Apply a bead of ointment about ½ in (1 c) long under the eyelid. Don't touch the eyeball directly with the tip of the tube!

Eyedrops and eardrops:
✔ When you administer eyedrops, hold the cat's head firmly from behind at the same time you pull back the lower eyelid with your index finger. Dribble a drop behind the lid with a dropper. Never touch the eyeball directly!
✔ When administering eardrops, carefully pull the ear out of the way and introduce four or five drops into the ear opening, then gently massage the base of the ear to distribute the fluid in the ear canal.

Giving Medicine

Tablets, pills, and capsules: Try to hide the pill in a tasty piece of food. Cut larger tablets into pieces and divide them up among several morsels. Sometimes you can outwit the cat; but if it's on to you, it may refuse the food. If so, try this: Hold the pill ready in one hand between thumb and forefinger while you grasp the cat's head behind the teeth with the other hand. The cat will involuntarily open its mouth. Then shove the pill as far as possible into the jaws and gently massage the throat in a downward direction until you feel the pill go down.

Push pills as far as possible into the throat.

Gently massage the throat until the pill is swallowed.

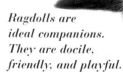

Ragdolls are ideal companions. They are docile, friendly, and playful.

Cat Associations

American Association of Cat
  Enthusiasts (AACE)
P.O. Box 213
Pine Brook, NJ 07058
(201) 335-6717

American Cat Association (ACA)
Dept. CF
8101 Catherine Avenue
Panorama City, CA 91402
(818) 781-5656

American Cat Fanciers
  Association (ACFA)
Dept. CF
P.O. Box 203
Pt. Lookout, MO 65726
(417) 334-5430

Canadian Cat Association (CCA)
Dept. CF
83 Kennedy Road, Unit 1806
Brampton, Ontario
Canada L6W 3P3

Other Organizations and Animal Protection Agencies

American Society for the
  Prevention of Cruelty to
  Animals (ASPCA)
424 East 92nd Street
New York, NY 10128
(212) 876-7700

Friends of Animals
P.O. Box 1244
Norwalk, CT 06856
(800) 631-2212
(For low-cost spay/neuter
program information)

The Humane Society of the
  United States (HSUS)
2100 L Street NW
Washington, DC 20037
(202) 452-1100

Pets Are Wonderful Support
  (PAWS)
P.O. Box 460489
San Francisco, CA 94146
(415) 241-1460
(Provides pet-related services for
people with AIDS)

Cat Magazines

Cats
P.O. Box 420240
Palm Coast, FL 32142-0240
(904) 445-2818

Cat Fancy
P.O. Box 52864
Boulder, CO 52864

Cat Fancier's Almanac
1805 Atlantic Avenue
P.O. Box 1005
Manasquan, NJ 08736-0805
(908) 528-9797

Catnip (newsletter)
Tufts University School of
  Veterinary Medicine
P.O. Box 420014
Palm Coast, FL 32142-0014
(800) 829-0926

Books for Additional Reading

Behrend, K. *Indoor Cats.*
  Hauppauge, New York: Barron's
  Educational Series, Inc., 1999.
Behrend, K. and Wegler, Monika.
  *The Complete Book of Cat
  Care.* Hauppauge, New York:
  Barron's Educational Series,
  Inc., 1991.
Daly, Carol Himsel, D.V.M. *Caring
  for Your Sick Cat.* Hauppauge,
  New York: Barron's Educational
  Series, Inc., 1994.
Frye, Fredric. *First Aid for Your
  Cat.* Hauppauge, New York:
  Barron's Educational Series,
  Inc., 1987.
Maggitti, Phil. *Guide to a Well-
  Behaved Cat.* Hauppauge, New
  York: Barron's Educational
  Series, Inc., 1993.
Viner, Bradley, D.V.M. *The Cat
  Care Manual.* Hauppauge, New
  York: Barron's Educational
  Series, Inc., 1993.
Wright, M. and S., Walters, eds.
  The Book of the Cat. New York:
  Summit Books, 1980.

The Author

Katrin Behrend is a journalist and animal book editor and author. She lives in Munich, Germany and in Italy. She has been a cat owner for many years.

The Translator

Eric Bye, M.A., is a freelance translator who works in German, French, Spanish, and English in his office in Vermont.

The Photographer

All photos are by Monika Wegler, except for: Monika Binder: Page 12 top right and below; page 14 top left, bottom right.

Monika Wegler is a professional photographer, journalist, and author of animal books. She concentrates on animal portraits and studies of behavior and movement of cats and dogs.

The Illustrator

György Jankovics, graphic artist, has illustrated numerous animal and plant books in this series.

Important Note

Make sure your cat has all its inoculations and is wormed (see pages 53 and 56); otherwise the health of the animal and humans could be jeopardized.

Some illnesses and parasites are communicable to humans (see page 54). You should consult your veterinarian any time your cat displays symptoms of illness (see page 55). Some people are allergic to cat hair. If you're not sure if you or any members of your family are, consult your doctor before getting a cat. You may be injured by bites and scratches in dealing with your cat. Have such injuries treated immediately by a doctor. Your cat can harm other people's property or even be the cause of an accident. Therefore it is important to have adequate insurance; in any case, you should carry liability insurance.

Cover and Inside Cover Photos

Front cover: Housecat. Back cover: Five-week-old kitten. Inside front: Bengal cat and her kitten. Inside back: Seven-week-old European Shorthair kittens.

Pages 2 and 3: Dog and cat. One heart and one soul
Pages 4 and 5: Abyssinian male cat stalking
Pages 6 and 7: Balinese, Redpoint, age four

English translation copyright © 1999 by Barron's Educational Series, Inc.
Original title of the book in German is *Katzen*
Copyright © 1998 Grafe und Unzer Verlag GmbH, Munich
Translation from the German by Eric A. Bye

All inquiries should be addressed to:
Barron's Educational Series, Inc.
250 Wireless Boulevard
Hauppauge, NY 11788
http://www.barronseduc.com

Library of Congress Catalog Card No. 99-12278
International Standard Book No. 0-7641-0933-2

Library of Congress Cataloging-in-Publication Data
Behrend, Katrin.
 [Katzen. English]
 Cats : everything about purchase, care, nutrition, grooming, and behavior / Katrin Behrend.
  p. cm. — (A complete pet owner's manual)
 Includes bibliographical references and index.
 ISBN 0-7641-0933-2
 1. Cats. I. Title. II. Series.
SF422.B44513   1999
636.8—dc21   99-12278
                                    CIP

Printed in Hong Kong
9 8 7 6 5 4 3 2 1

An expert answers the most frequently asked questions about owning a cat.

1 I'd like to have a cat, but I hesitate because I'd have to keep it in an apartment.

2 Can I expect my cat to be happy in an apartment after it's lived in a home where it gets plenty of exercise?

3 What should I look for in choosing a cat?

4 Should I get one cat or two?

5 Do I have to have my landlord's permission to own a cat?

6 Is it hard to know where you stand with a cat?

7 What should I do if my cat forgets to use the litterbox?

8 Shouldn't a cat have at least one litter of kittens?

9 Can an old cat get used to a new one?

10 Does a male cat that is allowed outdoors need to be neutered?